Forest Scientists

By Chuck Miller

Raintree Steck-Vaughn Publishers
A Harcourt Company

Austin · New York
www.steck-vaughn.com

Copyright © 2002, Steck-Vaughn Company

All rights reserved. No part of this book may be reproduced or utilized in any form or by any means, electronic or mechanical, including photocopying, recording, or by any information storage and retrieval system, without permission in writing from the publisher. Inquiries should be addressed to Copyright Permissions, Steck-Vaughn Company, P.O. Box 26015, Austin, TX 78755.

Published by Raintree Steck-Vaughn Publishers,
an imprint of Steck-Vaughn Company.

**Library of Congress Cataloging-in-Publication Data
is available upon request.**
ISBN: 0-7398-4751-1

Printed and bound in the United States of America
1 2 3 4 5 6 7 8 9 10 WZ 05 04 03 02 01

Produced by Compass Books

Photo Acknowledgments
Corbis, 32, 34; Bettmann, 16, 18, 25
Edward Bevilaqua, 20, 22
Luiz Claudio Marigo, 38-39
Photo Network/Bill Terry, title page; William Mitchell, 4
South Dakota Tourism, 40 (bottom)
Visuals Unlimited/John Lough, cover; Robert Perron, 9; Norris Blake, 10; Gary W. Carter, 12; C.P. George, 28, 41 (bottom); L. Bristol, 30, 40 (top); Larry Kimball, 41 (top)

Content Consultants
William H. Schlesinger
James B. Duke Professor of Biogeochemistry, Duke University, North Carolina

Maria Kent Rowell
Science Consultant, Sebastopol, California

David Larwa
National Science Education Consultant
Educational Training Services, Brighton, Michigan

This book supports the National Science Standards.

Contents

What Is a Forest Biome? .5

An Early Forest Scientist 17

A Scientist in United States' Eastern Forests . .21

A Scientist in the Indonesian Rain Forest 27

What Does the Future Hold for Forests? 35

Quick Facts 40

Glossary 43

Internet Sites 45

Useful Addresses 46

Books to Read 47

Index 48

These fern plants grow on the forest floor between large trees.

What Is a Forest Biome?

Many scientists study the forest **biome**. A biome is a large region, or area, made of communities. A community is a group of certain plants and animals that live in the same place.

Scientists study how different communities in a biome affect each other. Communities in the same biome are alike in some ways. In forests, for example, all plants and animals must be able to live among trees.

Forests are places with many trees and many kinds of plants and animals. People often think about trees and bears when they think about forests, but forests are home to many other living things besides trees and bears.

 This map shows where the different kinds of forests grow.

Where Are the Forests?

The three kinds of forests in the world are coniferous forests, deciduous forests, and rain forests. Coniferous forests are found in North America, Europe, and Asia. They are named after the **conifer** trees that grow there. Conifer trees grow cones that contain seeds and have needles instead of leaves. Most coniferous forests grow in cold climates where there is little rainfall.

Deciduous forests are found in North America, Russia, Europe, Japan, and Asia. They are named after the deciduous trees that grow there. Deciduous trees have leaves that change color and fall off every year, usually at the beginning of the cold season. The leaves grow back again, usually at the beginning of the warm season. Deciduous forests grow in mild climates where water is available in the form of rain or snow all year round.

Most rain forests are found near the **equator**. The equator is an imaginary line that wraps around the middle of Earth. Rain forests are named after their wet and rainy climate. They are warm places where many trees and plants grow close together.

Soil and Climate in Forests

Different forests have different kinds of soil. The leaves that fall from deciduous trees each year rot and mix into the soil. This makes soil in a deciduous forest good for plant growth.

The soil in coniferous forests and rain forests is not as good for plant growth. Soil in coniferous forests is often very sandy. Heavy rains in rain forests often wash away **nutrients** from the soil. Nutrients are materials that living things need to grow and stay healthy. Plants and trees in these forests have adapted to grow with few nutrients. To be adapted means that something is a good fit for where it lives.

Coniferous forests grow in a **climate** that is colder than the other forests. The cold season there is long. Temperatures are often below freezing during six months of the year. The warm season lasts only from 50 to 100 days.

Deciduous forests are warmer than coniferous forests. They receive more rain and have a longer warm season and a shorter cold season.

Rain forests have the hottest climate and receive the most rainfall of the forest biome.

▲ This moss has adapted to grow in the soil of this coniferous forest.

Some rain forests get up to 400 inches (1,016 cm) of rainfall each year. Some are very hot and receive heavy rains all year round. Others have dry seasons when it does not rain very much at all.

These epiphyte plants have adapted to grow on the sides of trees in the rain forest.

What Plants Live in Forests?

Plants have adapted to live in each kind of forest. Many plants and animals that live in each kind of forest could not live in an other biome.

Almost all coniferous forests have one or two kinds of conifer trees growing in them. These include spruce, pine, and fir trees. A few broadleaf trees, such as poplar, birch, and ash, also grow in coniferous forests. A broadleaf tree is a tree with wide leaves.

Most of the trees in deciduous forests are broadleaf trees. They include oak, maple, and elm. Shrubs, wildflowers, and moss also grow in deciduous forests.

Trees that grow in the rain forest include bamboo, mahogany, teak, palm, and fig trees. Vines and epiphytes are plants that can grow on other plants high above the ground.

Do you know which kind of forest has the most kinds of animals and plants living in it? It is the rain forest. The rain forest is home to more than one-half of the animal and plant species on Earth.

This flying squirrel has special flaps of skin to help it glide as it jumps from tree to tree.

What Animals Live in Forests?

Many kinds of animals live in deciduous and coniferous forests. Moose, deer, and elk are some of the **herbivores** that live there. Herbivores are animals that eat only plants.

Carnivores also live in these forests, including grizzly bears, wolves, and mountain lions. Carnivores are animals that eat only other animals for food. Tigers and jaguars are carnivores that live in the rain forests. They hunt the herbivores there, including monkeys and birds.

People live in all three kinds of forest. They have built villages, towns, and cities in the forests. The forests give people many of the things they need. Some people hunt the animals and catch the fish for food. Some people cut down trees and burn the wood to heat their homes. Others use the wood to build homes or make furniture. People also use plants from the rain forest to make medicine, clothing, and furniture.

This illustration shows how and why global warming happens.

Why Are the Forests in Danger?

Forests are necessary for a healthy world. Trees give Earth the oxygen that animals need to breathe. Trees also help stop rain, water, and wind from washing and blowing away, or **eroding**, soil. There are fewer nutrients in the soil where there are no forests.

People are harming the forests. Some people clear away the trees and plants from forests. Then, they build farms and roads where the forests were.

There are many logging companies cutting down trees in the rain forest. Logging is the business of cutting down trees to make them into lumber. Plants and animals that live in the rain forest are finding fewer places to live each year.

Global warming can also affect forests. Global warming is a slow rise in temperatures across Earth. Even small changes in temperatures can cause changes in weather patterns. These changes mean some forests might receive more or less rain and higher or lower temperatures than they are used to. These changes may affect some of the plants and animals that live in the forests.

Theodore Roosevelt (left) made Gifford Pinchot (right) the first Chief Forester of the United States.

An Early Forest Scientist

Gifford Pinchot was one of the first scientists who worked to save the forests of the United States. He was born in Connecticut in 1865 and spent his summers as a young boy in Connecticut with his family. The rest of the year his family lived in New York City.

In 1898, Pinchot became the head of the U.S. Division of **Forestry**. Forestry is the science of planting and taking care of forests.

Pinchot began telling newspaper reporters how important the forests were. People listened, and the U.S Forest Service was soon started. President Theodore Roosevelt named Pinchot its Chief Forester.

▲ Pinchot wrote about the importance of the forests, then shared his writings with others.

What Did Pinchot Do?

Pinchot wanted students in the United States to be able to study forestry. He thought the only way to do this was to show people how important the forests were to them. Pinchot taught people how a forest could affect them. He spent much of his time studying different forests and writing down what he saw. He taught people that forests are more than groups of trees. Forests have animals and plants living in them as well.

From Pinchot's writings, others began to see how important it was to study forests. Many U.S. schools started teaching forestry. Students went out into the forests to see and learn about what Pinchot had written. Pinchot started teaching forestry to students at Yale in 1910.

In 1898, there were 32 national forests. A national forest is a forest that is owned and protected by the government. As Chief Forester, Pinchot helped raise that number to 149 national forests by 1910. Almost 200 million acres (80 million ha) of U.S. forest were protected because of Pinchot's studies, writings, and work.

Pinchot and President Roosevelt also made "**conservation**" an important word in the United States. They said the word meant "to use natural resources wisely." Natural resources are materials found in nature that are useful to people.

Edward Bevilaqua is a scientist who works and studies in the forests of the eastern United States.

A Scientist in United States' Eastern Forests

Edward Bevilaqua works in the forests of the eastern United States. He is a forestry teacher at the State University of New York in Syracuse. He tries to see how soil, climate, and other trees will affect tree growth in the forest. He tries to figure out which trees will die and which ones will grow and why. In addition to studying trees in the United States, he has studied trees in Canada and in southern Brazil.

In the forests of the eastern United States, the climate changes often, says Bevilaqua. It can be sunny and very warm during the spring and summer months. It can rain and be cold at night, he says. The forest can also get very cold and snowy during the fall and winter months.

▲ Bevilaqua's students are doing field work by studying trees in the forest.

What Does Bevilaqua Do?

Bevilaqua drills holes into the side of trees to study them. He looks at the rings of wood on the inside of the trees. He uses these rings to understand how soil, climate, and other trees affect a tree's growth. Bevilaqua says that understanding how an entire forest grows can help people decide which trees to cut down. He says that this will help to preserve the forests.

Bevilaqua usually brings some of his students with him into the forests. They help him study the trees as part of their class work.

Bevilaqua once traveled to southern Brazil to help the people there learn how to use trees without cutting them all down. The people in southern Brazil need trees for building and to make paper. Bevilaqua helped them plant and farm eucalyptus trees. They used these fast-growing trees for wood and paper instead of using the slow-growing trees from the rain forest.

Bevilaqua has learned that wildfires can burn down an entire forest if the trees are too close together. The fire spreads more quickly then. Some scientists are burning down parts of forests on purpose so this does not happen, says Bevilaqua. Using fires on purpose to manage forests is called controlled burning.

Keeping Forests Healthy

The biggest threat to forests is people. The number of people in the world grows each year. More people means that more trees must be cut down to use for building materials. People will always need to cut down trees, says Bevilaqua. They must learn to do so in a way that allows both people and forests to keep living.

Bevilaqua says that forests are a very special biome. He says he can use a tree's rings to see what has happened to it in the past without guessing. He says forests are one of the few biomes that will allow him do this. If he can learn from the past, he can guess what will happen in the future. If he can do this, Bevilaqua says that he can help people learn how to use trees and save the forests.

Bevilaqua and his students are drilling a small hole into this tree to study its rings.

This map shows the location of the national park where Sri Suci Vtami works.

A Scientist in the Indonesian Rain Forest

Sri Suci Vtami is a scientist who works at the Ketambe Research Station on the Indonesian island of Sumatra. Sumatra is in the Pacific Ocean near southeast Asia. The research station is in a rain forest that is part of the Gunung Leuser National Park. Vtami has been studying the rain forest there for more than 10 years.

The Gunung Leuser National Park is one of the largest national parks in Indonesia. The Ketambe Research Station sits high up in the mountains of the park. There are two rivers near the rain forest that scientists must cross to get to the station.

▲ Vtami studies the ways orangutans use rain forest trees as shelter and as food.

What Does Vtami Do?

Vtami spends most of her time traveling through the rain forest and living in small huts. She works with her husband, Azwar, and other scientists from Indonesia and around the world. It rains almost all the time in the rain forest where Vtami works. The temperature can get cool there because of the rain. She has learned how to stay warm and not get lost when it rains.

Vtami studies orangutans that live in the Sumatran rain forest. Orangutans are part of the ape family. They have long, reddish brown hair and very long, strong arms. Orangutans live in Sumatra and only a few other places in the world. The orangutans Vtami studies live in the treetops of the rain forest. They do not live on the ground because they might be eaten by tigers and jaguars that live on the forest floor.

Vtami has been able to see the many ways orangutans use the trees in the rain forest. She says she has seen them use trees as medicine. The orangutans have learned to eat different parts of trees that will make them better if they are sick. Vtami has watched orangutans use sticks to dig bark off of trees to eat it. People are learning to make medicine from trees and plants in the rain forest, too, she says. Vtami was also the first person to see an orangutan eat meat. Most scientists had thought orangutans would only eat plants.

Logging companies cut down trees and sell the wood. People use it to build houses and furniture.

Keeping Rain Forests Healthy

Vtami says that all of the plants and animals in the rain forest are connected. They need each other to survive.

People are the biggest threat to the rain forests. The number of people living near rain forests grows each year. People cut down trees to use for building materials. They also hunt animals that live in the rain forests. Vtami thinks that the rain forests may be lost forever if people do not use them the right way.

What Are Other Kids Saying?

Rachel Runion is a 12 year old who lives near a deciduous forest. She says that there are so many things to do in forests that "you can never get bored." Rachel believes that we need to work to conserve the forest because "all the trees and plants give off shade, oxygen, and just plain beauty. Without those things, it would be a dull, boring, and tough world."

These kids are holding signs to remind people to help save the environment.

A Young Leader

Many young people know that forests are important to life on Earth. People and many plants and animals could not survive without them. Clint Hill was one such young person. He did not understand why people were polluting forests and other biomes, making them dirty with garbage or other things.

Clint started a club called Kids for Saving Earth (KSE). Thousands of children all over the world now belong to KSE. Their goal is to help save forests and other biomes in peaceful ways. KSE's website and address are listed in the back of this book.

One way kids in KSE help is by writing people who work in the U.S. Congress. These people can make laws that protect the forests in the United States. The kids in KSE first find out who represents them in Congress. Then, they can write to that person to tell him or her why it is important to protect Earth's biomes.

These people are practicing recycling. Recycling helps conserve forests.

What Does the Future Hold for Forests?

The future of the forests depends on the actions people take. People can help save the forests in many ways. **Recycling** is one way to help. Recycling means taking old things, such as empty cans, and using them to make new things. Many schools have recycling boxes. People can put paper they are done using in these boxes. This paper will be made into new paper without cutting down more trees.

People can also help forests by conserving the products that come from them. To conserve means to save. People can use less paper and wood that comes from trees. They can choose not to buy things that they know are made from trees in the rain forest.

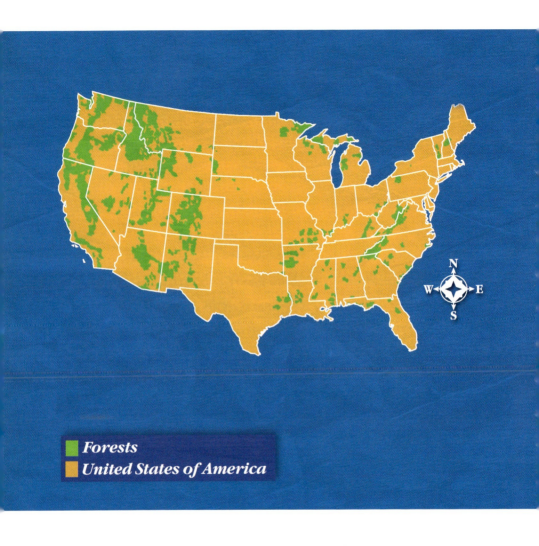

This map shows the location of the major national forests in the United States.

Where Are Forests Protected Best?

Forests are protected best in national parks. At many national parks, forests are protected from mining and logging.

In the United States, there are many national parks in forests people can visit, including Yellowstone National Park and Grand Teton National Park. Also, the Superior National Forest covers 3 million acres (1.2 million ha) of northeastern Minnesota. This coniferous forest was established as a national park in 1909.

Water covers more than 400,000 acres (160,000 ha) of the forest. The Boundary Waters Canoe Area is in the Superior National Forest. Many people canoe, hike, and camp there every year.

Did you know that forest plants can help make people well? Many medicines come from the plants in forests. In fact, most of the medicine used to treat cancer comes from plants in the rain forest. Scientists think the cures for many diseases will come from rain forest plants. They often go into rain forests to study the plants in the hope of finding more medicine.

The Endangered Jaguar

One endangered rain forest animal is the jaguar. Endangered means the animal is in danger of becoming extinct. People are the main cause of the jaguars' disappearance. The rain forest that jaguars once lived in has been cleared away for houses and farms.

Jaguars have also been hurt in other ways. People still hunt jaguars for their fur. Farmers living near rain forests sometimes kill jaguars because they think the jaguars will kill their cattle. Other people catch jaguars to keep as

▲ **The jaguar is an endangered species. There are very few of them left living in the wild.**

pets. In many places, it is against the law to kill a jaguar or to keep one as a pet.

Jaguars need people's help to survive. You can help by contacting one of the groups with an address or website listed in the back of this book. These groups help to teach people about saving the jaguar and other species.

Quick Facts

Fifty million acres (20 million ha) of rain forest are destroyed each year.

The rain forests in Southeast Asia have been the same for more than 70 million years.

One-quarter of the world's forests are deciduous.

One-quarter of the world's forests are coniferous.

One-half of the world's forests are rain forests.

Only 2% of the sunlight that hits the rain forest reaches through the trees and other plants to the rain forest floor.

Many endangered animals live in rain forests, including orangutans and jaguars.

Trees in a deciduous forest drop their leaves in the fall and winter to save energy. They grow them back in the spring and summer when the sun and climate give them more energy.

On the following pages, you can find sources of information that tell how to help save forests.

Glossary

biome (BYE-ohm)—large regions, or areas, in the world that have similar climates, soil, plants, and animals

carnivore (KAR-nuh-vor)—an animal that eats only other animals for food

climate (KLYE-mit)—the usual weather patterns in a place

conifer (KON-uh-fur)—an evergreen tree that produces cones

conserve (kon-SURV)—to save or protect something

deciduous (di-SIJ-oo-uhss)—trees that shed their leaves each year

equator (i-KWAY-tur)—an imaginary line around the middle of Earth, halfway between the North and South Poles

erosion (i-ROH-zhuhn)—when water, wind, or ice pick up and carry away Earth materials

forestry (FOR-ist-ree)—the science of planting and taking care of forests

herbivore (HUR-buh-vor)—an animal that eats only plants for food

nutrient (NOO-tree-uhnt)—something that is needed by living things to grow healthy and strong

recycling (ree-SYE-kuhl-ing)—to take old items, such as glass, plastic, newspapers, and aluminum cans, and use them to make new products

Internet Sites

Biomes/Habitats
http://www.allaboutnature.com/biomes
Find a description of each biome and information about the exciting animals that live there.

Educational in Nature: Forests
http://www.gp.com/EducationalinNature/topics/index.html
Learn more about the features of the different kinds of forests.

Kids for Saving Earth
http://www.kidsforsavingearth.org
Visit this site to learn about things you can do to help improve the environment.

National Park Service
http://www.nps.gov/
Explore the special features of different national parks and learn where each park is located.

Useful Addresses

American Forests
P.O. Box 2000
Washington, DC 20013

Canadian Wildlife Service
Environment Canada
Ottawa, Ontario
K1A 0H3

Kids for Saving Earth
P.O. Box 421118
Minneapolis, MN 55442

USDA Forest Service
P.O. Box 96090
Washington, DC 20090

Books to Read

Morgan, Sally. *Saving the Rain Forests.* New York: Franklin Watts, 1999.
Discover problems facing the survival of rain forests and different ways to save them.

Nelson, Julie. *Forests.* Austin, TX: Steck-Vaughn, 2000.
Explore the geography, animals, and plants of forests as well as people's effect on the biome.

Rutten, Joshua. *Forests.* Chanhassen, MN: Child's World, 1999.
Learn about forest features, such as the different plants and animals that live there.

Staub, Frank J. *America's Forests.* Minneapolis: Carolrhoda, 1999.
Find out about the different kinds of forests you can visit in the United States.

Index

Bevilaqua, Edward, 21-24
biome, 5, 11, 24, 33
broadleaf tree, 11

carnivore, 13
community, 5
coniferous, 6-8, 11, 13, 37
conservation, 19

deciduous, 6-8, 11, 13

epiphyte, 11

forestry, 17-19, 21

Hill, Clint, 33

jaguar, 13, 29, 38-39

logging, 15, 37

Pinchot, Gifford, 16-19

Roosevelt, Theodore, 16, 17, 19

soil, 8, 21

tree rings, 22, 24

Vtami, Sri Suci, 27-29, 31